SUMERIAN MYTHOLOGY

FOR KIDS

CHARLES MCKINNEY

DR.HISTORY

SUMERIAN MYTHOLOGY

Enchanting Ancient History and the Most Influential Events of Sumerian Mythology

FOR KIDS

CHARLES MCKINNEY

DR. HISTORY

Don't Forget Your Free Bonus Downloads!

As our way of saying thank you, we've included in every purchase bonus gift downloads. If you've enjoyed reading this book, please consider leaving a review.

Or Scan Your Phone to open QR code

Sumerian Mythology:

Enchanting Ancient History and the Most Influential Events of Sumerian Mythology for Kids

Copyright © 2023 by Dr. History

TABLE OF CONTENTS

INTRODUCTION

"As the sun rises, decisions are made. By the time the sun is up, kingship is conferred."
- Sumerian Proverb

Few cultures may legitimately claim to have had a part in the founding of civilization. One such civilization was ancient Sumer, which was established in the place known as Mesopotamia between the Tigris and Euphrates Rivers. Due to their enthusiasm for innovation, the Sumerians were credited with creating the first written language.

The Sumerians advanced the art of writing to a highly sophisticated level, even if they may have borrowed some ideas from earlier settlers. The cuneiform, one of the oldest writing systems in history, rose to prominence in the ancient Near East as the most crucial method of writing. Initially intended for record-keeping, the literature evolved into the creation of significant literary works such as mythologies and epics.

Myths were based on traditional tales. Some have a historical basis, while others are wholly made up. However, myths were more than just stories; they have deeper meanings in ancient and contemporary civilizations. Myths are renowned narratives that describe the universe and human existence.

The Sumerian's perception of the world was manifested in these mythologies. The origin of man and the world, birth, death, the afterlife, good and evil, and the essence of man himself are among the topics that reflect the common concerns of humanity throughout time. Ancient myths not only answered questions but also inspired people. The hero's journey is an example for young people as they take on adult duties. Some myths only provide comfort, such as those that attribute natural events to the deities rather than random occurrences of nature.

Myths are not necessarily happy stories, unlike fairy tales. The nature of myths is such that they are as frequently cautious as possibilities. They could frequently be sorrows as festivities, in keeping with the way of life. Many myths served as educational resources and social norms guides, addressing cultural and moral standards.

In the section below, we will discuss Sumerian mythology and learn how the ancient civilization viewed the world through their myths. We will also look into the origins of the myths and the culture that created them. Let us share the fascination in getting to know a civilization that seemed too advanced for its time.

ANCIENT CIVILIZATION IN HISTORY

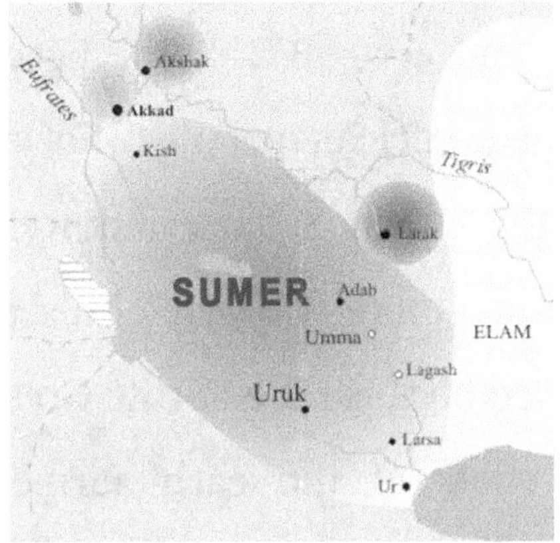

The Sumer map shows its city-states. Sumerian city-states, including Eridu, Bad-tibura, Shuruppak, Uruk, Sippar, and Ur, were among the most prominent ones.

The birthplace of Sumerian culture was southern Mesopotamia, currently Iraq, and Kuwait. Prior to the Babylonians, the Sumerians created the literary, religious, and agricultural systems that the Babylonians eventually changed and adopted. However, until the mid-19th century, hardly anyone speculated that such individuals and cultures existed. Moreover, it took a lot of work for historians and academics to understand and translate the discovered inscriptions.

The Sumerian's beginnings were unknown. The majority of academics believe that West Asian people who knew the Sumerian speech initially inhabited Sumer between approximately 5500 and 4000 B.C. Some have theorized that Sumerians were North African people who crossed into the Middle East from the Green Sahara and were in charge of establishing agriculture there. However, this proposition was frequently disregarded because the Fertile Crescent was highly implicated as the roots of the early farmers. The Fertile Crescent is a half-moon-shaped area of the Middle East. This area includes the modern states of Iraq, Syria, Lebanon, Israel, Palestine, and Jordan, as well as Kuwait's northern region, Turkey's southeast region, and Iran's western region.

Unlike Egypt, Assyria, and Babylonia, Western European scholars had access to a wide range of published information from the Bible and historical and post-classical references. In the Sumerians' instance, the scenario was unique. There was no tangible evidence of Sumer or its people and dialect in the Scriptural, historical, sand post-classical literary works. The exploration of the Sumerians and their speech was unforeseen.

The presence of the Sumerian vocabulary, individuals, and culture was ultimately validated after 50 years of translation and digging.

The Sumerians were non-Semitic, non-Indo-European immigrants that came to Mesopotamia from the East around 4000 B.C. to 3000 B.C. Semitic is most commonly used in reference to the Semitic languages. This description has been used since the 1770s to describe the language group now found in North and East Africa, Malta, and West Asia. They dwelt in Sumer, a comparatively tiny area between Tigris and Euphrates Rivers that extended northward from the Persian Gulf. The arrival of the Sumerians signaled the start of a two-millennium rivalry between Semites and Sumerians for control of the regions bounded by the two rivers.

Ancient Sumerians began to emerge in the Uruk era or 4th millennium B.C. This era was originally called after the Sumerian city of Uruk, which saw the onset of a modern way of life in Mesopotamia. Increased technological advancement, the significant progress of city aggregations with large architecture and political systems, and the spread of human culture throughout the Near East occurred during this period.

The term "Sumerian civilization" denotes a group of people who resided in cities or towns. They have also developed stable farming techniques comprising farm animals and have established a sociocultural hierarchy. The settlements that made up Sumerian cities were clusters of one- or two-story homes made from sun-dried bricks. It was eventually well-known that the Sumerians were the ruling cultural community in the Near East during the period between roughly 3500 and 2000 B.C.

It was the Sumerians who created and possibly discovered the cuneiform writing system. The Sumerian writing system is regarded as a significant turning point in the evolution of humanity's capacity to produce literary works, including prayers, ordinances, epic, narrative poems, and historical documents. Moreover, the Sumerians created and designed literary works full of substance and in a highly efficient form.

According to evidence, the Sumerians not only ruled the majority of Mesopotamia but also spread their influence to farther-off countries. The Sumerians made significant advancements in their financial, cultural, and governmental body during this time of colonial expansion and authority in the fourth millennium B.C. The establishment of spiritual and religious ideas went hand in hand with these advances. They also established a highly interconnected shrine coupled with spiritual and religious beliefs, which deeply affected all the inhabitants of the Near East.

The Semitic Accadian language progressively replaced Sumerian as the country's primary language after the Semites took over the city and overthrew Sumer by the end of the third millennium B.C. However, Sumerians remained to be utilized as the Semitic invaders' academic and liturgical language for many more decades to come, just like Greek did during the Roman era and Latin did throughout the Middle Ages. There is no doubt that the myths and ideas of Sumer were absorbed and significantly affected those of the entire Near East.

Fun Fact: *Counting backward in B.C.*

B.C. is an abbreviation for before Christ, and A.D. is for anno domini, a Latin word for during the Lord's year. The structure categorizes years according to a fundamental principle of when Jesus was born, with A.D. and B.C. indicating years after and before His birth, respectively. Dates in ancient times are frequently counted "backward," for example, 4000-3000 BC. This is because these periods occurred before 1 A.D. We are marking forward to 1 A.D. as there was no year "zero" technically.

Fun Fact: 3000 tablets.

The primary source materials for the research of Sumerian civilization were approximately three thousand tablets and remnants written in Sumerian and recorded around 1750 B.C. The stone tablets wherein Sumerian creations were embedded belonged to 2000 B.C. It was reduced by approximately 250 years, according to current studies that pointed to a date as low as 1750 B.C.

Trivia Questions:

1. Where is Mesopotamia in the present day?

2. When did the Sumerians come to Mesopotamia?

3. When was the Sumerian civilization discovered?

4. What writing system did the Sumerians invent?

5. How many clay tablets were the source materials for the Sumerian civilization research?

Answers:

1. Where is Mesopotamia in the present day? **Iraq and Kuwait**

2. When did the Sumerians come to Mesopotamia? **4000 B.C. to 3000 B.C.**

3. When was the Sumerian civilization discovered? **Mid-19th century**

4. What writing system did the Sumerians invent? **Cuneiform writing system**

5. How many clay tablets were the source materials for the Sumerian civilization research? **3000 clay tablets**

THE SUMERIAN DEITIES

A baked clay statue of the god Enlil is shown sitting. A now-lost object was held in the clenched left fist. There are visible remnants of red and black paint.

Gods and goddesses have significantly shaped how civilizations establish their norms, beliefs, and morality throughout history. People who served and followed gods were said to have been bestowed wealth, luck, and happiness in their lives. As several deities will be mentioned in the following sections, it is best to know first the significant Sumerian gods and goddesses.

The most powerful deity in the creation myth, An, presided over the religious gathering. An was in charge of the chronology and the seasonal changes, represented by the proper stars. An was the god of rulers as well. Then followed Enlil, the deity of winds and agriculture and the inventor of the hoe, described in the Sumerian literary works as a tool used in creation and destruction. The storm and the springtime breezes were perceived as Enlil's breaths and, subsequently, as his orders or mandates. Enlil also carried out the judgments of the sacred assembly.

The goddess Ninhursag, also known as Nintur or Ninmah, was on par with An and Enlil in terms of rank. She was the goddess of the rocky earth, which extended from the nearby mountainous region in the east to the barren desert with its fauna in the west. She was a deity of birth as well. She manifested as a distressed maternal animal weeping for her newborn foal son. Still, being the deity of birth, she is also the Mother of All Children, a maternal figure.

Enki was the god of the delectable waters of streams and wetlands, later known as Ea. He was the most innovative god and a master problem-solver. According to myth, Enki established country borders and allocated tasks to the gods. He was frequently prayed to by both gods and humans as a result. Damu, the son of Enki, served as the Girsu city's deity. He was the deity of flora, especially the sap that flows from trees and plants in the spring. The Ku'ara city god Asalluhc participated in purifying magic rites alongside the god Enki. He was reckoned as the son of Enki.

Enlil had sons, Nanna and Ninurta, from his relationship with the goddess Ninlil. Enlil was sent to Kur, the Sumerian underworld, due to seducing Ninlil. However, Ninlil pursued Enlil to the netherworld, where she was continually captivated by Enlil posing as different creatures. As a result, she bore him the netherworld beings Meslamtaea, Ninazu, and Ennugi. Ninurta was the deity of thunder and lightning, monsoon, and the hoe, whereas Nanna was the moon deity. The initial form of Ninurta was that of the storm cloud, which was pictured as a gigantic black bird hovering on expanded wings and roaring its thunderous cry from a lion's head. Ninurta's original name, Imdugud, means "rain cloud."

Meslamtaea, also known as Nergal, was referred to as the god of imposed death and was primarily linked to battle, sickness, and mortality. The goddess Ereshkigal, Nergal's wife, controlled the underworld together. Nergal did not play a significant role in epic poetry or mythologies. However, he did play a role in the Gilgamesh Epic and the Massive flood tale. Ninazu, on the other hand, was initially connected to serpents and plants but eventually developed the persona of a warrior god. In comparison, Ennugi was linked to the afterlife and farming, particularly irrigation.

Nanna and his wife, the goddess Ningal, had a daughter Inanna. The two essential deities, Ishkur and Utu, were also their sons. Ishkur was the weather deity, and Utu was the god of the sun and judgment. Ishkur possessed a dual nature because he was both the creator and demolisher of life. The field produced grain and other foods as a result of his rains. But as a consequence of his rage toward his enemies, severe weather brought demise, deprivation, and gloom.

The goddess of love, battle, and the morning star was Inanna. In the Sumerian divinities, she held a prominent position. Inanna was a fertility goddess who was also youthful, attractive, and passionate. However, she was never portrayed as maternal or a helper. She was incredibly well-known throughout the medieval Middle East. In many places of devotion, she likely superseded several regional goddesses. The unfortunate husband of Inanna was the herding deity Dumuzi.

The Sumerians believed a simple democratic social structure governed the gods. Experts had concluded that before the existence of humanity, the gods had to labor tirelessly on irrigation for agriculture and to dig out the Tigris and Euphrates grounds. They also established a landed nobility, with each deity managing and owning a property, the shrine, and his territories and directing the city in which it was situated. Property ownership was one of the royal privileges enjoyed by noblemen, known as landed nobility or aristocracy.

Fun Fact:

Highest god with a minor part. Despite being the supreme god in principle, An was a lesser figure in Mesopotamian myths, hymns, and sects. In addition to being the father of all deities, he was also the father of demons and wicked spirits. Frequently, he was portrayed with a horned headpiece as a symbol of power.

Fun Fact:

The love and war deity. A number of customs have been merged to create the figure of Inanna, the goddess of love and war. In other mythology, she is the wife or daughter of the sky deity An; in others, she is Nanna or Enlil's child. The goddess of coat, date palm, cereal crops, and provisions was how she was depicted in her early appearances.

Match Phrases:

Match the god to the relevant phrases about them.	
Inanna	The wind and agriculture deity
Erishkigal	The supreme god
An	The goddess of the underworld
Enki	The goddess of love and war
Enlil	The god of delectable waters

Answers:

Match the god to the relevant phrases about them.	
An	The supreme god
Enki	The god of delectable waters
Enlil	The wind and agriculture deity
Erishkigal	The goddess of the underworld
Inanna	The goddess of love and war

THE CREATION OF THE UNIVERSE AND MANKIND AND THE AFTERLIFE

The original Sumerian clay tablet of Inanna and Ebih. A clay tablet describing the conflict between the goddess Inanna and the mountain Ebih.

The most fundamental myths of a particular culture's holy traditions emerged and changed over time in an attempt to explain the creation of the universe, the reign of the gods, and the presence of man. Three main components made up Sumerian creation beliefs and principles in the third millennium BC- the formation and structuring of the universe and the creation of humankind.

Every culture has a creation myth that explains the beginning of the world and how everything came into being. Every creation myth acknowledges the existence of a divine power that was able to create the universe. According to many creation accounts, this supreme power was personified in god or a collection of gods, the Scripture being one example.

It was a long-held belief that heaven and earth were formerly in close proximity. The Sumerians believed in the universe as a sealed dome encircled by an ancient sea called Nammu. A netherworld and a large body of freshwater called the Abzu thrived beneath the continental earth, which served as the dome's core. The ancient sea, Nammu, conceived An and Ki.

An was the male deity representing the sky, while Ki, the earth goddess, represented the soil. Enlil, the god of rain, wind, and storm, was born as a result of An and Ki's union. An and Ki were torn apart by Enlil, who grew up to become the main god of the universe. Therefore, An, the deity of the heavens, took heaven. Enlil took his earth mother and usurped his father's sovereignty. Everything was working as planned. Enlil's marriage to his mother, Ki, laid the groundwork for the universe's structure, the birth of humanity, and the formation of culture. Ki was possibly associated with the goddess Ninhursag in ancient times.

The universe's establishment can thus be separated into earth and heaven. Heaven consisted of the sky and the space beyond, known as the "great above," where the sky god resided. The two parts that made up the earth were the land (exterior) and the "great below," which housed the netherworld or evil deities.

Due to the lack of available mythological information, heaven's structure was outlined as follows. Nanna was envisioned as traveling throughout the heavens in a gufa, bearing light to the dark deep blue sky. Initially utilized in Mesopotamia, the gufa was a straw-woven circular vessel that could be constructed from entwined thin branches. The "little ones" or the stars dispersed around him like grain. The "big ones," which might be the planets, followed him like a herd of untamed cattle. The Sumerian philosophers believed that the sun continued its trip to the underworld the night after sunset, transforming night into day. Moreover, on the twenty-eighth day of every month, the moon completes its day of rest in the underworld.

As for the composition of the earth, Enlil was responsible for establishing abundant sources and riches in the land by bringing seeds to the ground. Enlil created the pickaxe and, most likely, the plow as models for the agricultural tools that men would employ. He chose the farmer deity Enten as his loyal and dependable field assistant. Enki was more involved in the design of the earth, particularly the portion encompassing Sumer and its neighborhood. He delegated the numerous minor deities to their respective tasks and decided the destinies of Sumer, Ur, and Meluhha. Then, to make the land's livestock and cereal crops abundant, Enlil and Enki sent Labar, the cattle deity, and Ashnan, the goddess of the grain, from heaven to the earth.

As for the creation of men, Enlil made room for seeds to grow by removing heaven from the earth. He used the hoe he had made to crack the rough land at Uzumua. Innana had a place in Nippur called Uzumua. Nippur was an old Sumerian city. People sprouted from the hole Enlil's hoe created. Enlil made it possible for people to live on earth by separating heaven and earth.

Additionally, a poem served as the inspiration for another account of how man was created. The previous section mentioned that the gods had to work in the field. The poem describes that Nammu urged Enki to get out of bed and make helpers for the deities. Enki, the god of wisdom, considered the ability of the clay and the water of the depths to germinate. He instructed Nammu to have a few womb-goddesses tear off this fine-grained earth and have some noble creators strengthen it so she could form it or produce offspring to it. Humanity was hence made to free the gods from their labor.

The Sumerian afterlife was thought that dwellers carried on a shadowy form of earthly life in a gloomy, underground cavern. The goddess Ereshkigal was said to control this desolate realm known as Kur. A person's deeds in life had no bearing on how they would be regarded in the afterlife because all souls headed to the same place. However, burial evidence indicated that some individuals believed that the goddess

Inanna had the authority to bestow special favors on her followers in the afterlife. In the Third Dynasty of Ur, people thought that a person's fate in the next world relied on the manner in which they were buried. Those who had received lavish burials would be well-treated. In contrast, those who had received mediocre funerals would get on badly.

Fun Fact:

The resourcefulness of scholars. There were relatively few creation-related materials in the Sumerian stories. Therefore, scholars must look to the beginnings of stories and arguments to determine what was initially thought to be accurate. They looked into the first verses of a tale of a hero named Gilgamesh that made reference to the eras after the division of earth and heaven.

Fun Fact:

Sumerian Triad of Deities. The three most significant of the numerous Sumerian deities were An, the god of heaven; Enki, the water deity; and Enlil, the deity of the wind. The most divine trinity, An, Enlil, and Enki, embodied the three bands of stars that make up the sky's dome. In a scriptural setting, a triad of gods was typically not seen as one in the divine god or multiple facets of a specific god as in a Trinitarian.

Fill in the blanks to complete the story:

It was a long-held belief that _____ and ______ were formerly in close proximity. An was the male deity representing the ____, while ____, the earth goddess, represented the soil. ______ was responsible for establishing abundant sources and riches in the land by bringing seeds to the ground. He made room for seeds to grow by removing heaven from the earth. Enlil made it possible for _______ to live on earth by separating heaven and earth.

Answers:

It was a long-held belief that **heaven** and **earth** were formerly in close proximity. An was the male deity representing the **sky**, while **Ki**, the earth goddess, represented the soil. **Enlil** was responsible for establishing abundant sources and riches in the land by bringing seeds to the ground. He made room for seeds to grow by removing heaven from the earth. Enlil made it possible for **people** to live on earth by separating heaven and earth.

THE SUMERIAN DEVOTION

The Sumerian wind god Enlil's temple at Nippur, now known as Iraq, was a well-known place of pilgrimage in the fourth millennium BC. The Parthian era, which is thousands of years younger, is represented by the rectangular palace perched atop the ancient ziggurat.

The people's faith in the divine has influenced civilizations. It is simple to see how gods have shaped history, whether through the gods of Ancient Greece or Native American gods. It is the same with the followers of Christianity, Buddhism, Islam, or any other religion. No matter which god one believes in, dread of death, the afterworld, and divine power can affect how people live. In Mesopotamian culture, religion developed into homogenous, clear, and consistent customs that changed over time in response to its internal requirements for understanding and representation. People's lives were entirely influenced by religion, which also affected social order and authority.

Religious activity had various stages of progress between the fourth and third millennia B.C. It is logical to assume a fundamental basis of worship of natural forces, frequently represented by nonhuman forms, especially those directly relevant to primary economic activities. In the fourth millennium B.C., many of these sculptures were of fertility divinities with aspects of mortality and rebirth. They displayed different characteristics depending on whether they were fertility deities revered by marsh inhabitants, orchard producers, herders, or farm owners. During the early third millennium B.C., religious practice evolved. It became a perception of the gods as resembling humans and a caste system of early democracy where each deity had specific roles and duties. A class distinction based on birth is known as a caste system.

The inhabitants of Sumer, the earliest educated civilization in prehistoric Mesopotamia, practiced the Sumerian religion.

The Sumerians believed their deities were responsible for all orders in nature and society. Mesopotamia was organized into tiny groups known as "city-states," each had a large city and its surrounding countryside. Divinely-guided priests and religious leaders virtually governed the city-states before Sumerian kingship began.

As per cultic beliefs, humankind achieved its purpose by meeting the material desires of the deities. Consequently, they built temples for the gods in abundant fertile regions, serving as the deities' homes. Like many other sacred sites in ancient Mesopotamia, the temple's main goal was to guarantee the god's presence and to offer a location where he might be addressed.

Early Sumerian temples were fundamental, single-room buildings that occasionally stood on raised platforms. The city's ruler was also responsible for the temple dedicated to the local deity. The ruler's consort oversaw the city goddess' temple. In contrast, the gods regarded as the offspring of the city god and goddesses had their temples managed by the ruler's children. The god existed in the temple but was not contained, through a statue made of priceless wood and covered in gold. People made offerings for this statue as well as cooked meals each day. These offerings were harvested from the temple's fields. Fishermen or farmers delivered them as a tribute to the temple.

According to Sumerians, gods, and people lived in the same world. The gods dwelt among mortals in temples on their vast estates. They reigned, defended ordinance and peace for humanity, and waged war for humankind. In general, there was no room for uncertainty when it came to recognizing and executing the will of the gods. Humankind desired flawless performance of their cult's rituals and eager and competent labor on their properties. They also expressed disapproval of violations of the law and morality.

Fun Fact: *Festivals are held monthly.*

The significant monthly festivals and a handful of special events provided a break from the everyday routine. A sudden requirement to perform the complex ceremony for cleansing the ruler may arise on such special occasions. Almost frequently, among the festival events were instances when the ruler or other worshippers expressed their requests and prayers along with the right gift.

Fun Fact: *3Divination practices.*

There were instances when humans were uncertain if they were doing god's will. They used divination to ask the gods for guidance in these situations. Simply put, the gods may act independently and express particular desires through visions, signals, or prophecies. Resting in the temple, hoping that god would deliver an illuminating dream, was the most popular method of divination.

Questions:

1. How were gods represented in the fundamental basis of worship of natural forces? Why do these gods display different characteristics?

2. How did religious practice evolve during the 3rd millennium B.C.?

3. How did Sumerians ask for a god's guidance?

4. What are temples, and who was responsible for them?

Answer:

1. How were gods represented in a fundamental basis of worship of natural forces? Why do these gods display different characteristics? **Non-human forms represented them. Gods display different characteristics depending on their worshippers, such as marsh inhabitants, orchard producers, herders, or farm owners**

2. How did religious practice evolve during the 3rd millennium B.C.? **Gods were perceived in human forms**

3. How do Sumerians ask for a god's guidance? **Through divination practice**

4. What are temples, and who was responsible for them? **Temples were fundamental, single-room buildings that served as homes for the deities. The city's ruler was responsible for the temple.**

HOLY SITES OF WORSHIP

Iraq's Great Ziggurat of Ur, located 21 kilometers southwest of Nasiriyah, has undergone numerous reconstructions. The old capital of Sumeria was Ur.

In the previous section, temples were undoubtedly a fundamental part of the Sumerian religion. Let us further discuss in detail how temples were made, which would reflect the Sumerian's devotion to their gods and goddesses.

People practicing religion may do so in outdoor shrines, private homes, or little, distinct chapels in the city's residential areas. However, the temple was the most esteemed location. According to archaeology, the temple can be dated to the earliest settlement phases. From the Early Dynastic period onward, it was evident that the temple served as the god's home or place of residence, as described by the Sumerians.

A temple would often be constructed on several asymmetrical synthetic structures stacked one atop the other. These temples were squared-shaped to build a ziggurat by the end of the third millennium B.C. The temple's cookhouse, workrooms, and other similar spaces were all encompassed by a substantial wall on the lowest of these platforms.

The god's residence was on the uppermost level, accessible through a stairwell. It was positioned in the inner chamber, a rectangular space with an entry door in the long wall close to one corner. The god's seat was on a pedestal in a recess at the end of the narrow wall farthest from the entrance. Sitting statues of pilgrims were along the two long walls, and a fireplace in the center heated the floor. A drape protecting the deity from impure eyes appeared to have been supported by low columns in front of the god's seat. The deity would have a desk, a bedroom, and a bath in an adjoining room. The statue would be dressed in lavish clothing, given a wash, and led to the god's bedroom for the night.

The gods had a staff of household servants. These priests had trained extensively in cooking, baking, serving, and bathing. They also obtained music training so they could play music during the gods' feasts and sing adoration. In times of difficulty and sadness, there were also elegists to comfort. An elegist is a person who writes mourning songs or sorrowful poems that grieve the deceased.

The god's existence was ensured by providing a place to live, food, and services. Additionally, his presence was guaranteed by a fitting personification (the statue) and, for some rituals, the ruler's body. Greeting offerings, worship songs as introductions to pleas, and other gestures were used to persuade the deity to welcome the worshiper and hear and receive their requests.

The infrastructure created for the gods and the size of the territory they owned and farmed was of vital importance. Therefore, it was inevitable that temples would compete for commercial significance with comparably large royal estates. The temple also has the ability to generate significant storable reserves that it could use to counteract bad years thanks to a properly-maintained estate. Additionally, the temple's manufacturing facilities, such as its weaveries, allowed it to take and use portions of the population. This included the widowed, homeless, prisoners, and other individuals who, in the absence of the temple, would not have survived or might turn into a danger to the neighborhood.

Fun Fact: *Ziggurats.*

The principal towns of Mesopotamia were known for their ziggurats, which were pyramid-shaped temple towers with stairways. It was typically square or rectangular, with an average of 50 meters square (or 40 50 meters) at the foundation, and lacked any interior compartments. There are roughly 25 ziggurats that may be identified, evenly distributed among Assyria, Babylonia, and Sumer.

Fun Fact: *Astrology.*

Various cultures have used astrology in multiple ways since Sumerian times. Astrology was closely tied to investigating extraordinary events in nature or culture, but it was far more systematic. The Sun, Moon, and planets' motions and appearances were thought to reveal information about upcoming events that would influence the country or, in some circumstances, the individual's destiny.

Complete the Sentences

1. The ________ was the most esteemed location for worship.

a. private homes   b. temple   c. mountains

2. The god's residence was on the uppermost level, accessible through a __________.

a. stairwell   b. ancient elevator   c.forklift

3. The gods had a staff of _________ servants.

a. church   b. household   c. field

4. __________ were pyramid-shaped temple towers with stairways.

a. temple   b. ziggurats   c. city-states

5. The _______ existence was ensured by providing a place to live, food, and services.

a. ruler's   b. people's   c. god's

Answers:

1. The **temple** was the most esteemed location for worship.

b. temple

2. The god's residence was on the uppermost level, accessible through a **stairwell**.

a. stairwell

3. The gods had a staff of **household** servants.

b. household

4. **ziggurats** were pyramid-shaped temple towers with stairways.

b. ziggurats

5. The **god's** existence was ensured by providing a place to live, food, and services.

c. god's

LITERARY HERITAGE OF MYTHS AND EPICS

Ancient Sumerian cuneiform clay tablet. Cuneiform writing, in particular, was done on clay tablets as a writing tool.

Most of our understanding of Sumerians comes from artifacts discovered in Mesopotamian city mounds since the 19th century. The literary documentation was of crucial relevance, which consisted of texts inscribed in cuneiform (wedge-shaped) script on clay tablets or, for notable reasons, on stone tablets. The especially religious texts, which include deity lists, myths, psalms, lamentation, petitions, rituals, prophetic texts, invocations, and other forms, are at heart.

The Sumerians, whose oldest written documents dated from the mid of the 4th millennium B.C., were the founders of Mesopotamian literature. It is the world's most senior recorded work of literature. Internal indicators also suggested that recording its songs and tales in writing predates and likely lived alongside a lengthy oral-literary heritage. Furthermore, the types of primary literature may have evolved from these oral traditions.

The main body of literature and its oral predecessors were initially written for artistic and amusing reasons. Its primary objective in ancient Mesopotamia was improving what was regarded as advantageous. The main genres were formal expressions of appreciation, except for literary works of wisdom. Additionally, praise's magical ability is to call forth, teach, or stimulate the virtues it suggested. The mystical quality of literature may have disappeared from awareness in earlier times. It gave way to more essentially artistic perspectives that welcomed the narrative forms of myth and epic for the enjoyment of the story and the values communicated. Both poetically and otherwise, the praise songs were seen as expressions of obedience and devotion.

Epics, mythologies, and songs were all thought to uphold underlying strengths and virtues through adoration. However, laments were initially intended to celebrate lost gifts and abilities in an effort to resurrect them magically. This reappearance was accomplished by utilizing the power of an intense outpouring of longing for the lost blessings and strengths and their clear representation.

The Sumerians originated the main literary styles of Mesopotamian literature as oral works. The beginnings of writing, which were first documented in the middle of the 4th millennium B.C., were mostly logographic. Logographic writing was a method in which each term or morpheme was represented by one diagram or symbol. It was a severely flawed method of portraying the spoken word for a long time. As writing became more precise during the third millennium B.C., more verbal compositions appeared to have been written down. With the 3rd dynasty of Ur, a significant amount of literary works had emerged, supplemented by a younger generation of talented writers.

Myths are affirmations that narrate and applaud heroic deeds in ancient Mesopotamian literary works. These actions have specific rather than universal significance in the oldest Sumerian myths. It was reasonable, considering that they dealt with the authority and acts of one particular god with a specific area of influence in the universe. These myths included Dumuzi's Death, Inanna's Descent, and the Engendering of the Moon god and his Brothers. Most of these mythologies were based mainly on fertility religious sects. They regarded either the absence of nature's fertility with the commencement of the dry season or food storage below the ground.

Fun Fact: *The literary form of epics.*

Epics originated more recently than myths in general. "Gilgamesh and Aga of Kish, " a brief Sumerian epic narrative, was told in primary epic form. It described Gilgamesh's triumphant uprising against his tyrannical ruler and former ally, Aga of Kish. The tales of "Enmerkar and the Lord of Aratta," "Enmerkar and Ensuhkeshdanna," and "Lugalbanda Epic," all featured rulers of the first dynasty of Uruk as heroes, were more in the romantic epic style.

Fun Fact: *The cuneiform script has been utilized for over 3000 years.*

Cuneiform, a Latin name that translates to "wedge-shaped," was created by the Sumerians probably around 3400 B.C. It was made up of several hundred symbols utilized by ancient writers to form words or units of speech on damp clay tablets using a reed pen. The cuneiform was initially invented to record daily economic transactions and keep accounting and evolved into a whole writing system applied to poems, archives, ordinances, and literary works.

Match the Words with the Literary Terms:

1. Expressions of obedience and devotion
2. To celebrate lost gifts and abilities
3. Narrate and applaud heroic deeds
4. A term was represented by one diagram or symbol

Literary Type:

Myths, Epics, Logographic, Lamentations, Praise Songs, Poems

Answers:

1. Expressions of obedience and devotion – **Praise Songs**

2. To celebrate lost gifts and abilities - **Lamentations**

3. Narrate and applaud heroic deeds - **Myths**

4. A term was represented by one diagram or symbol – **Logographic**

BATTLES FOR POWER IN SUMER

A remnant of Sumerian brickwork. This ziggurat at the ancient Sumerian city of Kish, east of Babylon, Iraq, was built of red, burnt bricks, as is evident.

The First Dynasty of Kish was the first governing group in Sumer with historical support. Etana of Kish was the first king to be mentioned. He was credited with endowing all the lands in a historical source. Gilgamesh, king of Uruk, who assumed power at approximately 2700 B.C., was the most well-known of the early Sumerian emperors. He is still known for his fictitious achievements in the Epic of Gilgamesh.

A power conflict that broke out between the rulers of Kish, Erech, and Ur, sometime about 2600 B.C., resulted in the region's rulers somewhat playing "musical chairs" over the following 400 years. Following the first battle, the kingdom of Awan took over. It relocated the governing body beyond Sumer until the domain was returned to the Kish. The Kish temporarily retained power before Enshakushanna, King of the Uruk, rose to power.

Following the short reign of King Enshakushanna, the Adabian conqueror Lugalannemundu ruled for 90 years and was believed to have extended his empire to the Mediterranean. Lugalannemundu defeated the Gutian people, who subsequently came to control Sumer. In 2500 B.C. Kubaba ascended to the throne. After a brief reign by Unzi, the first ruler of the Akshak Dynasty, Puzur-Suen, Kubaba's son, established the fourth Kish dynasty. The final Kish period lasted for a century until Lugal-zage-si, king of Uruk, ruled for 25 years. Sargon then took power in 2234 B.C.

Sargon's history, an Akkadian, was veiled in stories, some of which were started by Sargon himself, as others attest. The

Akkadians took their name from Akkad, the city they founded. Akkad was a historical territory in what is now central Iraq. Following that triumph, Sargon seized Ur, Umma, and Lagash and established himself as the monarch. His military rule extended as far as the Persian Gulf.

Sargon constructed the city of Agade, South of Kish, as his base. Agade developed into a significant harbor and ancient center. Sargon's army, regarded as the first structured professional army in history and the first to utilize chariots in battle, was also based in Agade. By elevating his daughter Enhedu-anna to the chief priestess position of Ur's moon god cult, Sargon gained control of the religious traditions of the Akkadians and the Sumerians. People often associate her with the duplications of temple hymns, which Enheduanna also penned and recorded in her writings.

After Sargon's death, his son Rimush encountered a massive revolt and was assassinated. Sargon reigned for 50 years. Manishtushu, Rimush's brother, suffered the same fate. In 2292 B.C., Naram-Sin, Sargon's grandchild, ascended to the throne. Serving as the final Akkadian ruler was Sharkalisharri, the son of Naram-Sin. The Gutians attacked in 2193 BC. Their time was characterized by dispersed turmoil and disregard. The magnificent metropolis of Agade fell into ruin and vanished from history during the Gutian era.

In 2100 BC, Utuhegal, king of Ur, conquered the Gutians. It was the last triumph of the leadership of Sumer. Ur-Nammu, the previous governor of Ur, ascended to the throne after Utuhegal's brief rule. He began a monarchy that would govern for around a century before the Elamites invaded Ur and seized power. Elamites were the people that lived in Elam, also known as the Highlands, located east of Babylon. In present-day Iran's extreme west and southwest, a civilization known as Elam once existed.

Fun Fact: *The only female Sumerian ruler.*

Most early Sumerian kings were listed by name on a clay tablet known as King List, along with information about how long they reigned. The list featured Sumer's sole female queen and an odd mingling of historical fact and myth. Her name was Kubaba, and she was believed to have ascended to the throne of the city-state of Kish sometime around 2500 B.C

.

Fun Fact: *Sargon's past*

King Sargon was said to have been the hidden child of a high priestess who threw him out into a river in a basket. This tale was subsequently used for Moses in the Old Testament. According to Sumerian legend, Sargon was the son of a groundskeeper who advanced to the rank of cupbearer for Ur-Zababa, king of Kish. A cupbearer was equivalent to a senior official position rather than a servant one.

True or False:

1. The First Dynasty of Ur was the first governing group in Sumer with historical support.

2. A power conflict broke out between the rulers of Kish, Enlil, and Enki sometime in about 2600 B.C.

3. The Adabian conqueror Lugalannemundu ruled for 190 years and was believed to have extended his empire to the Mediterranean.

4. Kubaba was the only female Sumerian ruler.

5. The Akkadian, Sargon, then took power in 2234 B.C.

Answers:

1. The First Dynasty of Ur was the first governing group in Sumer with historical support. **False. First Dynasty of Kish**

2. A power conflict broke out between the rulers of Kish, Enlil, and Enki sometime in about 2600 B.C. **False. Erech and Ur**

3. The Adabian conqueror Lugalannemundu ruled for 190 years and was believed to have extended his empire to the Mediterranean. **False. 90 years**

4. Kubaba was the only female Sumerian ruler. **True**

5. The Akkadian, Sargon, then took power in 2234 B.C. **True**

PEOPLE OF OTHER CULTURES MIGRATING TO SUMER

The power conflict within Sumer and, eventually, the invasion of other civilizations seriously impacted Sumerian culture. Outside invaders defeated the kingdom and its culture. Sumer had already perished as a political institution, and Sumerian was already an extinct dialect by the conclusion of the third millennium B.C.

The prevalence of Old Akkadian peaked under Sargon the Great's leadership, from 2334 to 2279 B.C., in the Akkadian Empire. Despite that, the majority of governmental tablets were still penned in the scribes' language, Sumerian. For over a thousand years, the standard dialects of Akkadian and Sumerian coexisted. But by 1800 BC, Sumerian had evolved into a literary language mostly known to scribes and academics.

Although Sumer was reclaimed by Sumerian leaders, due to

the rise of Akkadian-speaking Semites in Assyria and other places, the territory was beginning to sound more Semitic than Sumerian. Further, Semitic Martu (Amorites) waves arrived in the south. They established rival local powers like Isin, Larsa, Eshnunna, and Babylonia. The Amorites were a prehistoric Northwest Semitic-speaking people from the Levant who also controlled a sizable portion of southern Mesopotamia.

Amorite tribes moved significantly between 2100 and 2001 B.C., presumably due to a prolonged drought. They invaded southern Mesopotamia. Early Mesopotamian literature from Sumer, Akkad, and Assyria, to the west of the Euphrates, portrayed them as primitive and wandering people. They played a part in the collapse of the Third Dynasty of Ur. The Amorites were depicted as chief-led nomadic tribes who pushed their way into areas where they had to provide for their herds.

As the Third Dynasty's centralized government gradually fell apart, neighboring northern territories started to reestablish their prior independence. Further, other city-states and districts in southern Mesopotamia also joined the movement. Elam's soldiers were simultaneously invading the dynasty from the south of Iran, making Sumer more susceptible. Several Amorite chieftains in southern Mesopotamia fiercely exploited the crumbling empire to gain control for themselves.

Apart from outsiders invading Sumer, coincidentally, the inhabitants of southern Mesopotamia significantly shifted northward at the same time. The shift was due to agricultural problems. Growing salinity was adversely compromising the farm output of the Sumerian lands. In this area, soil salinity has long been acknowledged as a severe issue. In dry climates with significant levels of evaporation, irrigated soils without proper drainage gradually built up with soluble salts, drastically lowering agricultural productivity.

Wheat agriculture switched to more salt-tolerant barley during the Akkadian and Ur III periods. However, more was needed to prevent the population from declining by around three-fifths between 2100 B.C. and 1700 B.C. This significantly changed the power dynamics in the area, diminishing Sumerian-speaking districts while increasing those where

Akkadian was the dominant language. Sumerians would, therefore, only be used for scholarly and religious purposes, just like Latin was used in medieval Europe.

The Amorites ruled Sumer after an Elamite occupation and siege of Ur under the reign of Ibbi-Sin, roughly 2028–2004 B.C. The Sumerian king list refers to the autonomous Amorite nations of the 20th to the 18th centuries as the "Dynasty of Isin." The same dynasty ended with the establishment of Babylonia under Hammurabi in 1800 B.C.

Fun Fact: *The largest city in the world.*

By the fourth millennium B.C., there were perhaps a dozen city-states founded by the Sumerians. Major Sumerian city-states encompassed Eridu, Ur, Nippur, Lagash, and Kish. However, one of the earliest and largest was Uruk. It was a prosperous trading center with around 40,000 and 80,000 people and six miles of protective walls. The biggest settlement in the world when it reached its height around 2800 B.C.

Fun Fact: *The Sumerians were seasoned traders who traveled frequently.*

The Sumerians were compelled to establish one of the earliest land-and-sea commerce channels since their native country lacked lumber, stone, and mineral resources. They traveled to Dilmun (presently Bahrain), Anatolia, Lebanon, Oman, and Indus Valley, and they may have even reached Afghanistan.

Reflection Question:

The Sumerian civilization was crumbling, mostly due to conflicts among leaders of the Sumerian city-states. Outside invaders took advantage of the situation. Consequently, people of other cultures migrated to Sumer. However, the Sumerians themselves were simultaneously moving northwards due to agricultural problems. Wheat agriculture switched to more salt-tolerant barley during the Akkadian and Ur III periods. However, the effort was not enough to prevent the population decline. **Do you agree? Yes/No**

ORIGINATOR OF MYTHOLOGIES

The Sumerians were highly resourceful individuals who established several technologies. Additionally, they could take innovations from other fields and use them on a far larger scale. Their innovations included the hoe, wheel, and writing (the cuneiform system). The Sumerians' creation of writing was one of Mesopotamia's most significant achievements. The Sumerian legends and myths were a foundation and inspiration for the design of its conqueror's tales.

When Akkadian replaced Sumerian as the primary tongue used in Mesopotamia, it was not without its literary heritage. According to the characteristics of the Akkadian orthography, writing was first adopted by the Sumerians quite early. The Sumerian academic concepts and patterns were partly responsible for developing the myths and epics in Akkadian literature around the 19th century B.C. Further, the Akkadian myths are in several respects reliant on Sumerian elements; however, they handle older Sumerian ideas and forms with originality and a broader scope.

Rich civilizations were formed in Sumer and Akkad. The descendants of the Sumerians and Akkadians, the Amorites, a western Semitic tribe that had ruled all of Mesopotamia by about 1900 B.C., acquired this cultural inheritance. The Tigris-Euphrates region's political and economical center was Babylon during the Amorites' dominion, which lasted until roughly 1600 B.C. The vast Babylonian empire included the entire southern Mesopotamia and a portion of northern Assyria.

The Sumerians made a very outstanding contribution to the development of literary principles. They were credited with creating the earliest pieces of literature ever written. Despite being written in Sumerian, the contents significantly impacted academic development. Other civilizations, including the Babylonians, Hittites, Assyrians, and Persians, quickly adopted this cuneiform writing system to communicate.

Even though Sumerian as a dialect ultimately disappeared, its writing system survived and was borrowed and subsequently modified by numerous neighboring cultures. The Epic of Gilgamesh, the oldest known piece of literary work, and the influence of cuneiform on other dialects and writing systems were the two main contributions of Sumerian works of literature.

Further, the Sumerians left behind a significant number of written documents; however, they are best known for their epic poetry. This literature profoundly impacted subsequent Greek and Roman writers and portions of the Bible, particularly the tales of the Great Flood, Eden, and the Tower of Babel.

Apart from literature, Sumerians also have an influence on religion. The religious records of any era, especially older times, are a concise summary of prior generations. They must be carefully evaluated and put in the proper perspective before being assessed. The religion of the succeeding Mesopotamian inhabitants was greatly affected by Sumerian beliefs. This included Hurrian, Akkadian, Babylonian, Assyrian, and other Middle Eastern cultural ties, all keeping aspects of Sumerian religion in their myths and faiths. This was because the ancient Mesopotamians were highly traditional in religious affairs and hesitant to let go of anything of a sacred past.

Further, the Sumerians first made many of the most significant discoveries, creations, and ideas that we take for granted today. They created time by partitioning each day and night into 12-hour intervals, each hour into 60 minutes, and minute into 60 seconds. They also established the first irrigation systems, the first education systems, the initial interpretations of the Great Flood story and other scriptural tales, the earliest epic, the structure of government, and magnificent buildings.

Fun Fact: *The Epic of Gilgamesh was based on a true story.*

The protagonist of the Gilgamesh Epic was possibly an actual historical figure from Sumerian history. Although the poem's protagonist was a demigod with Herculean power, most academics thought he was modeled on a real king who reigned as Uruk's fifth king. The historical Gilgamesh, assumed to have lived approximately 2700 B.C., was mentioned in the Sumerian "King List."

Fun Fact: *Mathematics and Measurements.*

Today, people still utilize Sumerian measurements and math. Today's mathematics is rooted in the number ten, whereas Sumerians primarily used a sexigesimal system based on clusters of 60. Base-60 inevitably became obsolete, although its influence may still be seen in the minute and hour measurements. Other traces of the Sumerian sexigesimal system can be seen in geometric dimensions like the 12 inches in a foot and the 360 degrees in a circle.

Circle the Correct Word:

1. The Sumerians were highly resourceful individuals who established several **technologies/writing systems.**

2. The Sumerians' creation of **irrigation/writing** was one of Mesopotamia's most significant achievements.

3. Rich **civilizations/literature** were formed in Sumer and Akkad.

4. The Epic of Gilgamesh was based on a **fictional/true** story.

5. Apart from literature, Sumerians also have an influence on **agriculture/religion.**

Answers:

1. The Sumerians were highly resourceful individuals who established several **technologies.**

2. The Sumerians' creation of **writing** was one of Mesopotamia's most significant achievements.

3. Rich **civilizations** were formed in Sumer and Akkad.

4. The Epic of Gilgamesh was based on a **true** story.

5. Apart from literature, Sumerians also have an influence on **religion**.

CONCLUSION

"The strength of my god completes my own."

- Sumerian Proverb

The relevance of myths today is no different than it was in history. Myths provide age-old explanations and act as a compass for successive generations. The concepts and protagonists of myths are everlasting and endlessly relevant. They are recreated and adapted to each younger generation's lives, adding another level of fiction and fact to the tales.

Mythology is included in large part in any person's heritage. It serves as a permanent reminder of our origins and identity. Myths, stories, and folktales - every civilization has its own. Moreover, several widely practiced religions have their roots in mythology, another reason why mythology is significant. These specific myths are accounts of conflicts between good and evil. Such tales can be found in every religion, both traditional and contemporary.

In today's modern world, mythology is still important. The valuable life lessons from these myths are still adaptable even to this day. Further, mythology is especially prevalent in today's fantasy novels. To cite a few examples, J.K. Rowling's Harry Potter has its own legend. In contrast, The Chronicles of Narnia by C.S. Lewis is filled with personas from Greek and Roman mythology. The main character, or hero, must face off against the antihero or villain. During that adventure, the hero learns important morals and principles that will help him defeat the bad guy.

The fact that mythology is still relevant is that it is simple storytelling. Everyone enjoys telling a compelling story or listening to someone else tell a great story.

The Sumerian innovations influenced the development of culture throughout the greater Fertile Crescent. Even after the Sumerians vanished from history, their creations continued to influence kingdoms, empires, and nations. On the other hand, the prominence of Sumerian as a literary language is demonstrated by the fact that interpretations were rarely permitted to remove the original Sumerian words.

BIBLIOGRAPHY

- The original Sumerian clay tablet of Inanna and Ebih. A clay tablet describing the conflict between the goddess Inanna and the mountain Ebih.

  "File: Tablet describing goddess Inanna's battle with the mountain Ebih,Sumerian - Oriental Institute Museum, University of Chicago - DSC07117.JPG" by Daderot is marked with CC0 1.0. To view the terms, visit https://creativecommons.org/publicdomain/zero/1.0/deed.en?ref=openverse.

- Ancient Sumerian cuneiform clay tablet. Cuneiform writing, in particular, was done on clay tablets as a writing tool.

  Sumerian Cuneiform Clay Tablet" by Gary Lee Todd, Ph.D., is marked with CC0 1.0. To view the terms, visit https://creativecommons.org/publicdomain/zero/1.0/?ref=openverse.

- The Sumer map shows its city-states. Sumerian city-states, including Eridu, Bad-tibura, Shuruppak, Uruk, Sippar, and Ur, were among the most prominent ones.

  "File: Sumer map.jpg" by ca:Imatge:Umma2350.png is licensed under CC BY-SA 3.0. To view a copy of this license, visit https://creativecommons.org/licenses/by-sa/3.0/?ref=openverse.

- A baked clay statue of the god Enlil is shown sitting. A now-lost object was held in the clenched left fist. There are visible remnants of red and black paint.

  "File: God Enlil, seated, from Nippur, Iraq. 1800-1600 BCE. Iraq Museum.jpg" by Osama Shukir Muhammed Amin FRCP(Glasg) is licensed under CC BY-SA 4.0. To view a copy of this license, visit https://creativecommons.org/licenses/by-sa/4.0/?ref=openverse.

- The Sumerian wind god Enlil's temple at Nippur, now known as Iraq, was a well-known place of pilgrimage in the fourth millennium BC. The Parthian era, which is thousands of years younger, is represented by the rectangular palace perched atop the ancient ziggurat.

  "Temple of Enlil" by D-Stanley is licensed under CC BY 2.0. To view a copy of this license, visit https://creativecommons.org/licenses/by/2.0/?ref=openverse.

- A remnant of Sumerian brickwork. This ziggurat at the ancient Sumerian city of Kish, east of Babylon, Iraq, was built of red, burnt bricks, as is evident.

  "Sumerian Brickwork" by D-Stanley is licensed under CC BY 2.0. To view a copy of this license, visit https://creativecommons.org/licenses/by/2.0/?ref=openverse.

- Iraq's Great Ziggurat of Ur, located 21 kilometers southwest of Nasiriyah, has undergone numerous reconstructions. The old capital of Sumeria was Ur.

  "Great Ziggurat of Ur" by D-Stanley is licensed under CC BY 2.0. To view a copy of this license, visit https://creativecommons.org/licenses/by/2.0/?ref=openverse.

About Us

At our core, we believe that history is more than just a subject to be learned. It's an experience to be had.

Our mission is to educate and inspire the next generation by providing them with a window into the fascinating and often surprising world of the past. We want to help young people make sense of the complexities of history and understand the lessons it has to offer.

By creating unforgettable encounters with relics of the past, we hope to ignite a lifelong passion for learning and discovery.

Thank you,